Division Search

Directions: Divide to solve the problems in the problem list. Circle the problem and write - and =. The first one has been done for you

Problem List

- [ ] 10 ÷ 2 = 5
- [ ] 21 ÷ 3 =
- [ ] 16 ÷ 2 =
- [ ] 9 ÷ 3 =
- [ ] 6 ÷ 2 =
- [ ] 24 ÷ 3 =
- [ ] 18 ÷ 2 =
- [ ] 30 ÷ 3 =
- [ ] 14 ÷ 2 =
- [ ] 15 ÷ 3 =
- [ ] 4 ÷ 2 =
- [ ] 6 ÷ 3 =
- [ ] 22 ÷ 2 =
- [ ] 18 ÷ 3 =
- [ ] 24 ÷ 2 =
- [ ] 12 ÷ 3 =
- [ ] 8 ÷ 2 =
- [ ] 27 ÷ 3 =
- [ ] 20 ÷ 2 =
- [ ] 36 ÷ 3 =

21	7	20	21	8	22	14	2	7	1
3	12	14	15	2	21	14	22	22	2
7	18	9	9	4	1	24	16	5	18
14	4	2	2	28	2	3	9	45	3
15	8	4	4	29	3	8	25	3	6
18	2	9	8	30	4	7	27	3	5
16	28	2	49	24	2	12	3	16	4
17	12	10 ÷ 2 = 5			5	3	9	2	6
12	3	4	27	38	6	33	1	8	7
6	3	2	6	4	15	32	20	22	23
1	34	18	13	36	3	20	2	21	30
16	9	3	3	3	5	11	10	20	3
2	3	4	5	12	7	7	21	6	10
22	2	11	15	20	8	6	2	3	27

Division Search

Directions: Divide to solve the problems in the problem list. Circle the problem and write - and =. The first one has been done for you

Problem List

- [ ] 16 ÷ 4 = 4
- [ ] 30 ÷ 5 =
- [ ] 28 ÷ 4 =
- [ ] 15 ÷ 5 =
- [ ] 32 ÷ 4 =
- [ ] 20 ÷ 5 =
- [ ] 48 ÷ 4 =
- [ ] 10 ÷ 5 =
- [ ] 36 ÷ 4 =
- [ ] 40 ÷ 5 =
- [ ] 24 ÷ 4 =
- [ ] 25 ÷ 5 =
- [ ] 12 ÷ 4 =
- [ ] 45 ÷ 5 =
- [ ] 8 ÷ 4 =
- [ ] 50 ÷ 5 =
- [ ] 52 ÷ 4 =
- [ ] 35 ÷ 5 =
- [ ] 40 ÷ 4 =
- [ ] 60 ÷ 5 =

15	5	3	4	25	5	5	30	33	31
12	13	14	15	52	53	54	32	4	8
24	4	6	6	7	8	9	10	11	12
2	4	6	8	30	12	13	10	5	2
50	5	10	7	5	2	8	9	8	24
3	20	2	9	6	33	4	14	4	20
4	23	40	18	6	10	2	17	3	5
5	24	5	27	40	4	10	33	60	4
16	25	8	32	9	48	4	12	5	2
÷4	25	13	12	8	21	9	32	12	52
=4	26	45	4	46	45	5	9	1	4
12	27	3	3	10	6	13	36	31	13
13	35	22	13	12	32	28	4	7	5
36	4	9	10	35	5	7	48	49	50

Division Search

Directions: Divide to solve the problems in the problem list. Circle the problem and write - and =. The first one has been done for you

Divide by 6 & 7

Problem List

- [ ] 21 ÷ 7 = 3
- [ ] 72 ÷ 6 =
- [ ] 28 ÷ 7 =
- [ ] 54 ÷ 6 =
- [ ] 14 ÷ 7 =
- [ ] 84 ÷ 6 =
- [ ] 42 ÷ 7 =
- [ ] 60 ÷ 6 =
- [ ] 35 ÷ 7 =
- [ ] 48 ÷ 6 =
- [ ] 56 ÷ 7 =
- [ ] 24 ÷ 6 =
- [ ] 84 ÷ 7 =
- [ ] 12 ÷ 6 =
- [ ] 63 ÷ 7 =
- [ ] 18 ÷ 6 =
- [ ] 49 ÷ 7 =
- [ ] 36 ÷ 6 =
- [ ] 70 ÷ 7 =
- [ ] 30 ÷ 6 =

12	28	7	4	7	80	63	7	9	4
11	9	20	49	7	7	41	48	17	5
35	18	17	34	8	30	4	21 ÷ 7 = 3		
7	27	56	7	8	12	13	14	15	6
5	35	2	20	4	14	2	40	1	7
14	28	72	43	10	7	4	60	10	84
15	88	6	28	7	2	12	6	7	7
16	33	12	22	47	21	12	10	3	12
18	6	3	32	36	6	6	8	20	10
9	34	44	70	33	13	84	6	14	20
42	7	6	7	24	15	16	17	18	30
21	24	6	10	6	12	16	12	6	2
22	85	86	87	4	9	30	6	5	40
48	6	8	72	76	70	32	54	6	9

Color by Code Division

Directions: Color the picture by dividing the numbers. Use the chart below to determine the color of each shape.

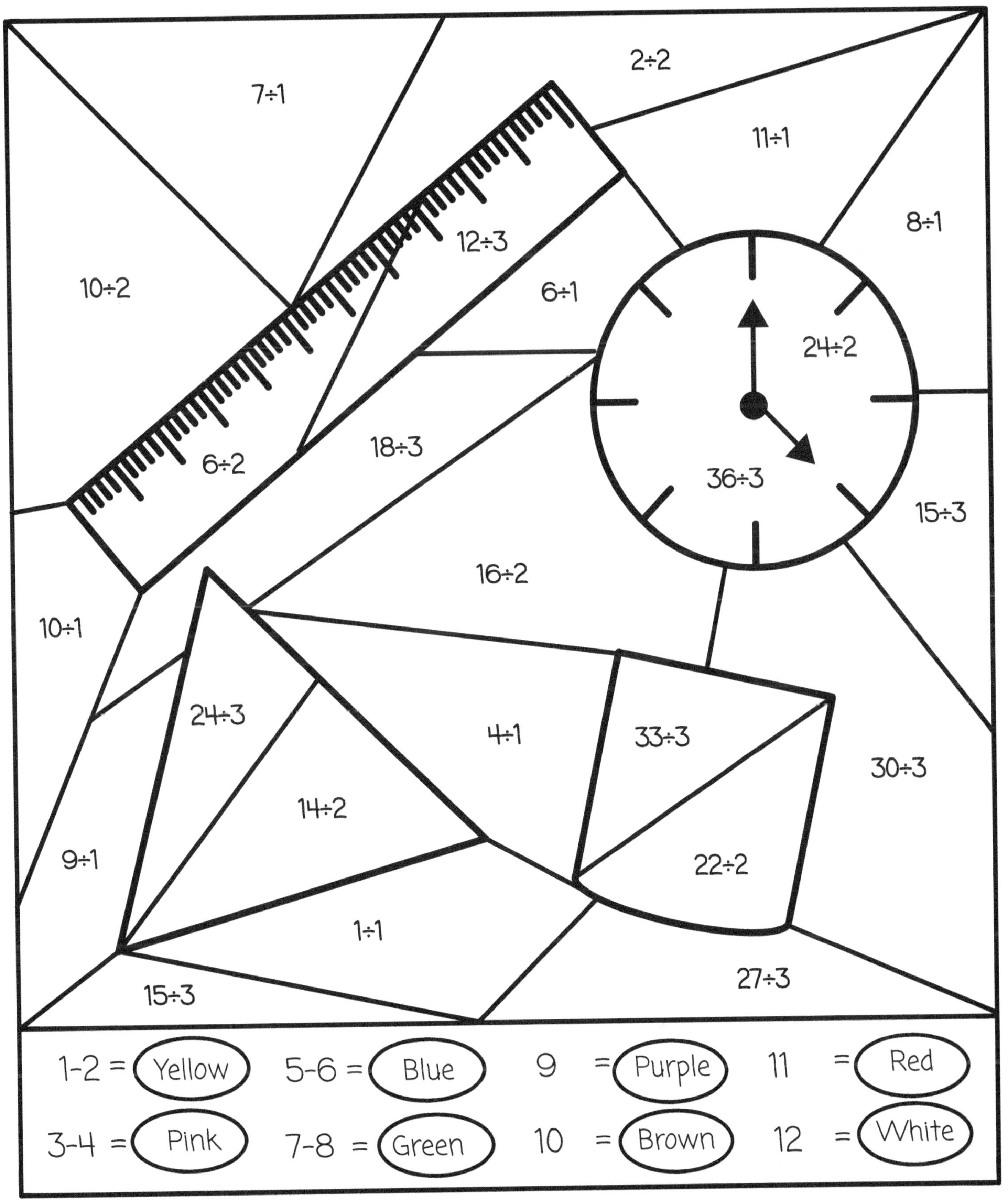

Division Search

Directions: Divide to solve the problems in the problem list. Circle the problem and write - and =. The first one has been done for you

Problem List

- [ ] 80 ÷ 8 = 10
- [ ] 27 ÷ 9 =
- [ ] 120 ÷ 8 =
- [ ] 18 ÷ 9 =
- [ ] 72 ÷ 8 =
- [ ] 45 ÷ 9 =
- [ ] 88 ÷ 8 =
- [ ] 36 ÷ 9 =
- [ ] 64 ÷ 8 =
- [ ] 54 ÷ 9 =
- [ ] 96 ÷ 8 =
- [ ] 63 ÷ 9 =
- [ ] 24 ÷ 8 =
- [ ] 81 ÷ 9 =
- [ ] 32 ÷ 8 =
- [ ] 126 ÷ 9 =
- [ ] 16 ÷ 8 =
- [ ] 90 ÷ 9 =
- [ ] 40 ÷ 8 =
- [ ] 108 ÷ 12 =

100	27	10	20	30	40	50	81	9	9
122	9	20	73	7	45	9	5	44	10
107	3	30	74	8	30	4	21	45	11
25	27	54	9	6	12	108	18	120	12
30	35	2	75	9	14	9	9	46	36
72	8	9	76	10	7	12	2	10	9
90	88	6	126	9	14	12	6	82	4
16	8	2	77	11	64	8	8	83	3
20	40	3	124	40	8	5	12	90	2
57	120	8	15	12	13	32	13	9	24
88	80	65	129	16	25	8	15	10	8
8	24	96	8	12	12	4	16	6	3
11	85	86	121	4	9	80 ÷ 8 = 10			1
58	63	9	7	11	22	33	55	55	4

Color by Code Division

Directions: Color the picture by dividing the numbers. Use the chart below to determine the color of each shape.

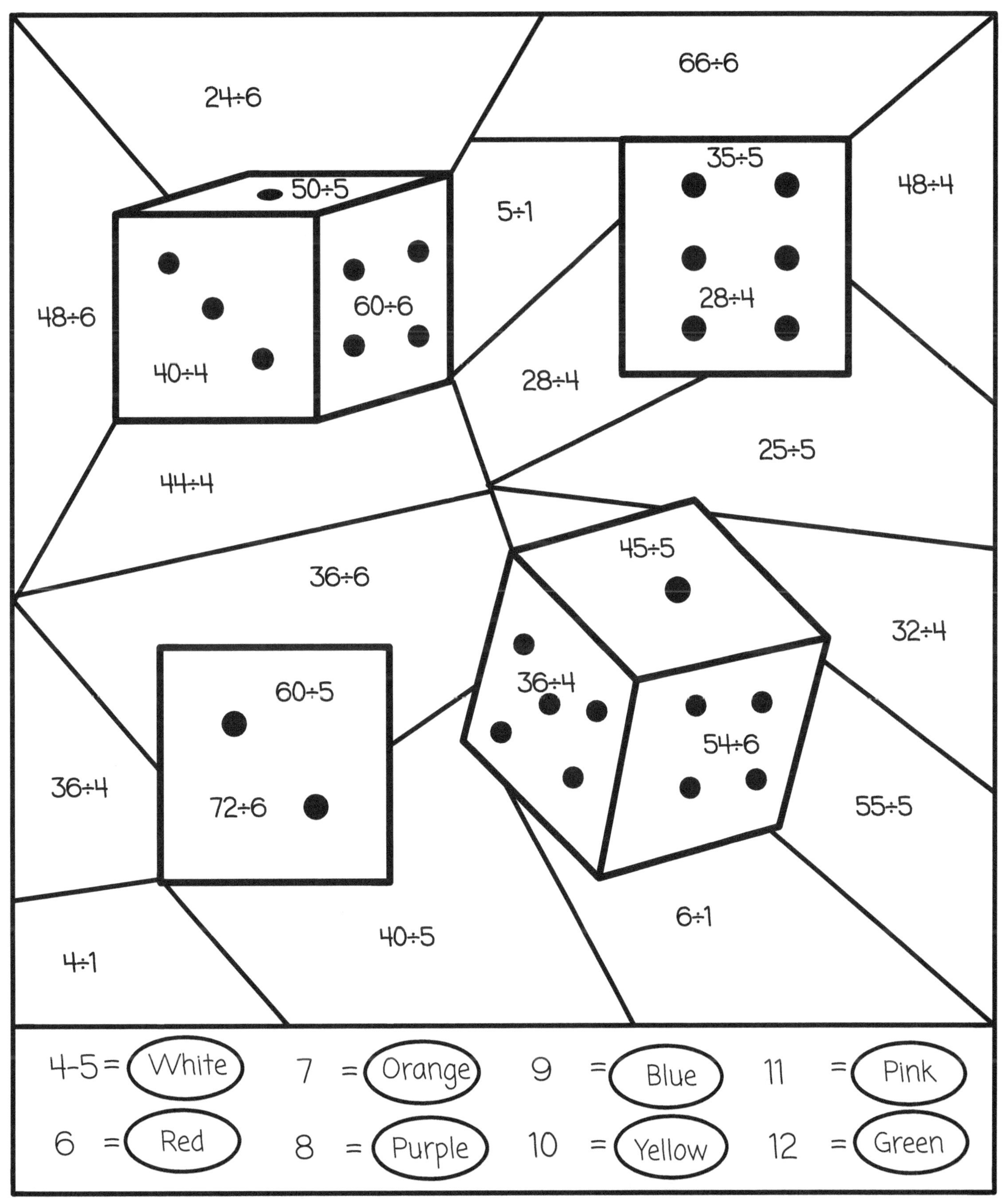

COLOR BY CODE DIVISION

Directions: Color the picture by dividing the numbers. Use the chart below to determine the color of each shape.

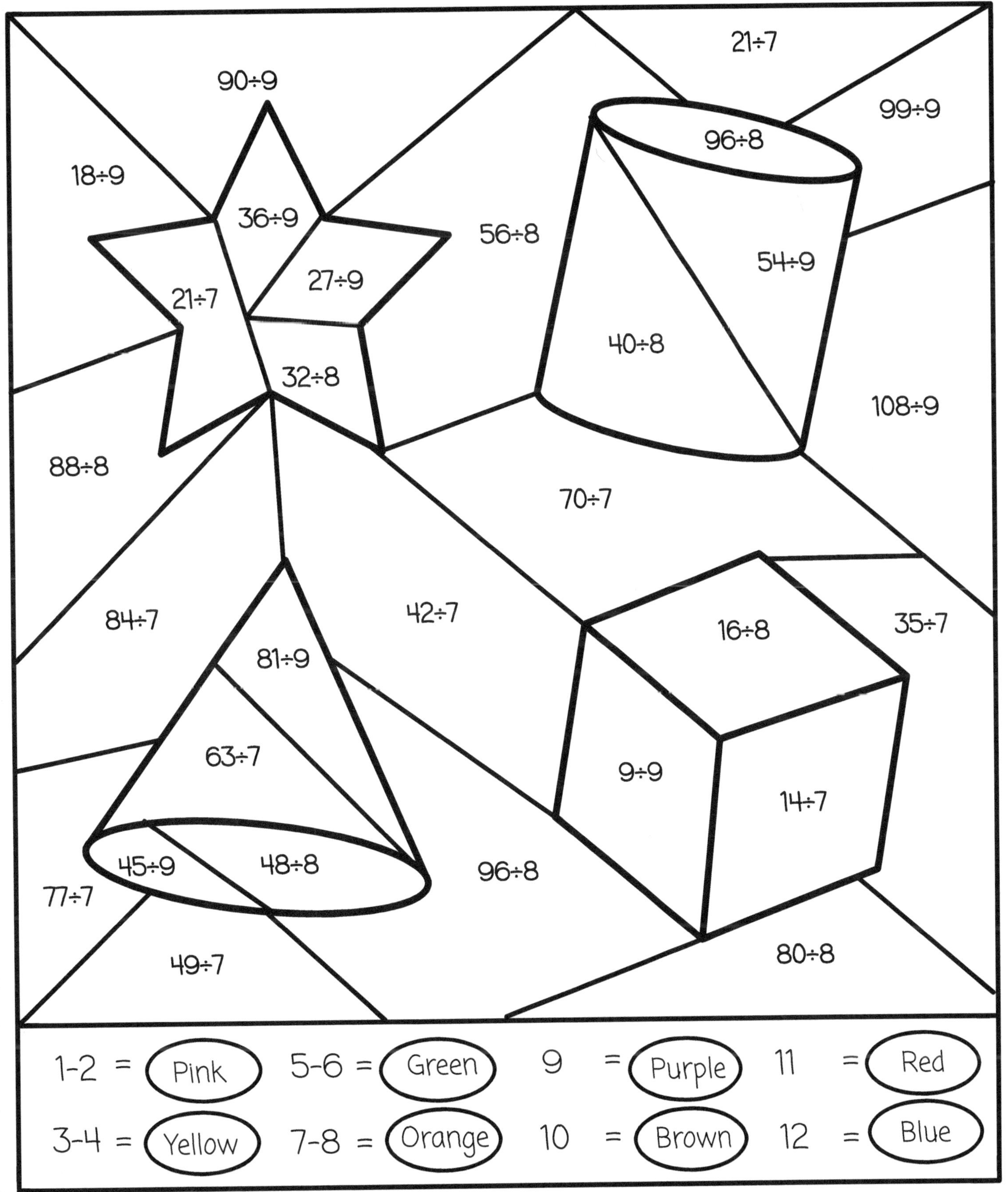

COLOR BY CODE DIVISION

Directions: Color the picture by dividing the numbers. Use the chart below to determine the color of each shape.

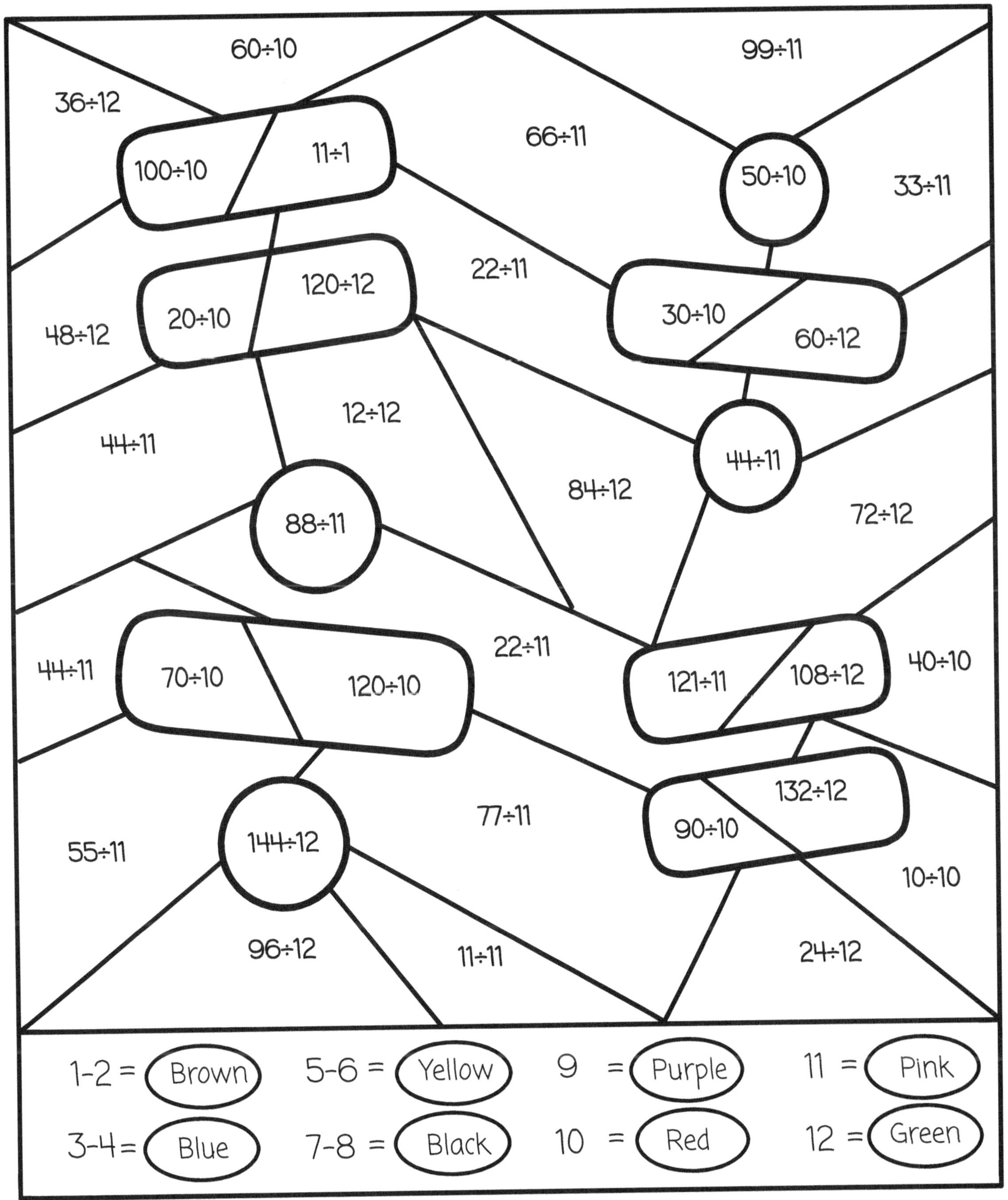

Division Circles

Divide the inner number to get the outer numbers

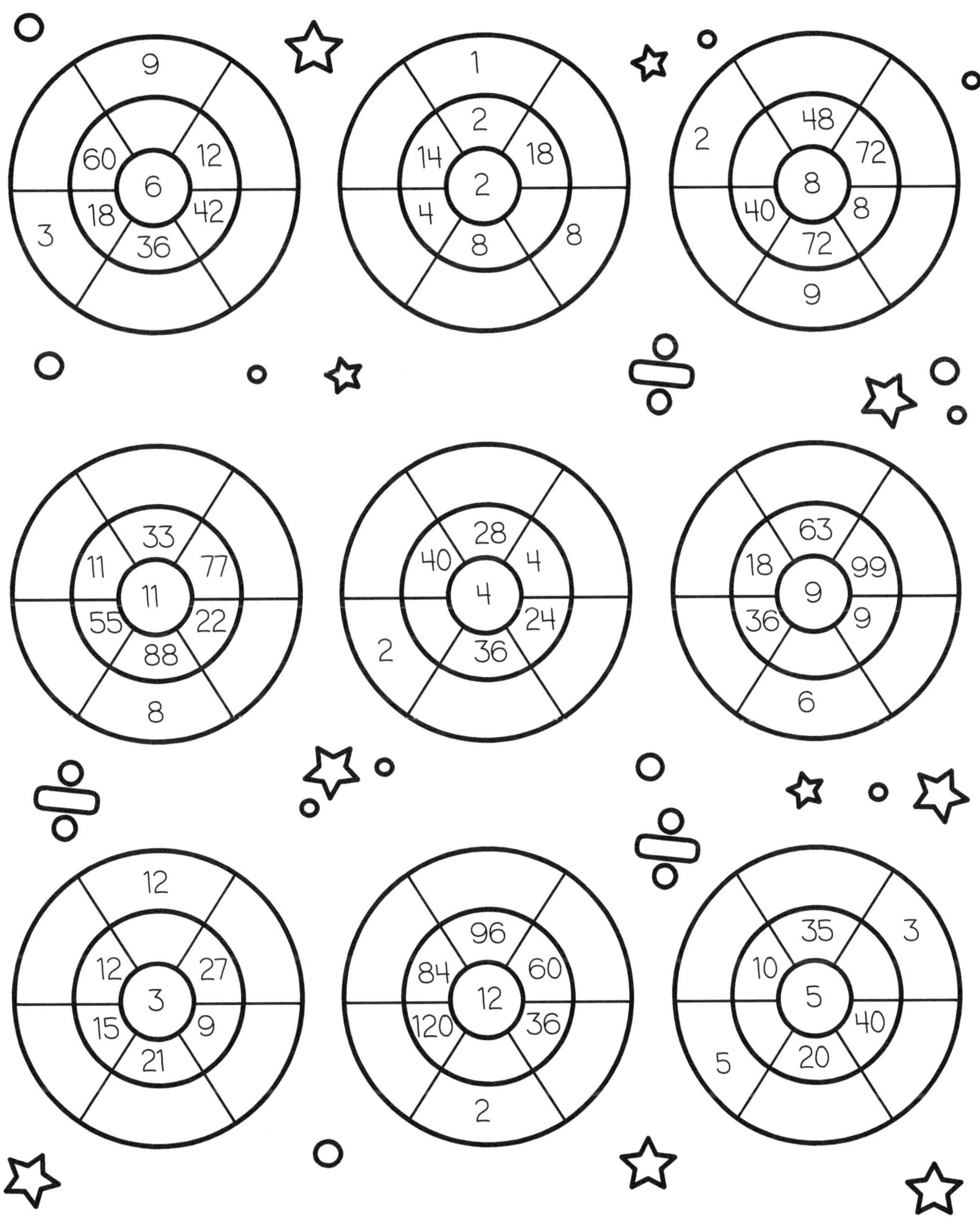

Division Circles

Divide the inner number to get the outer numbers

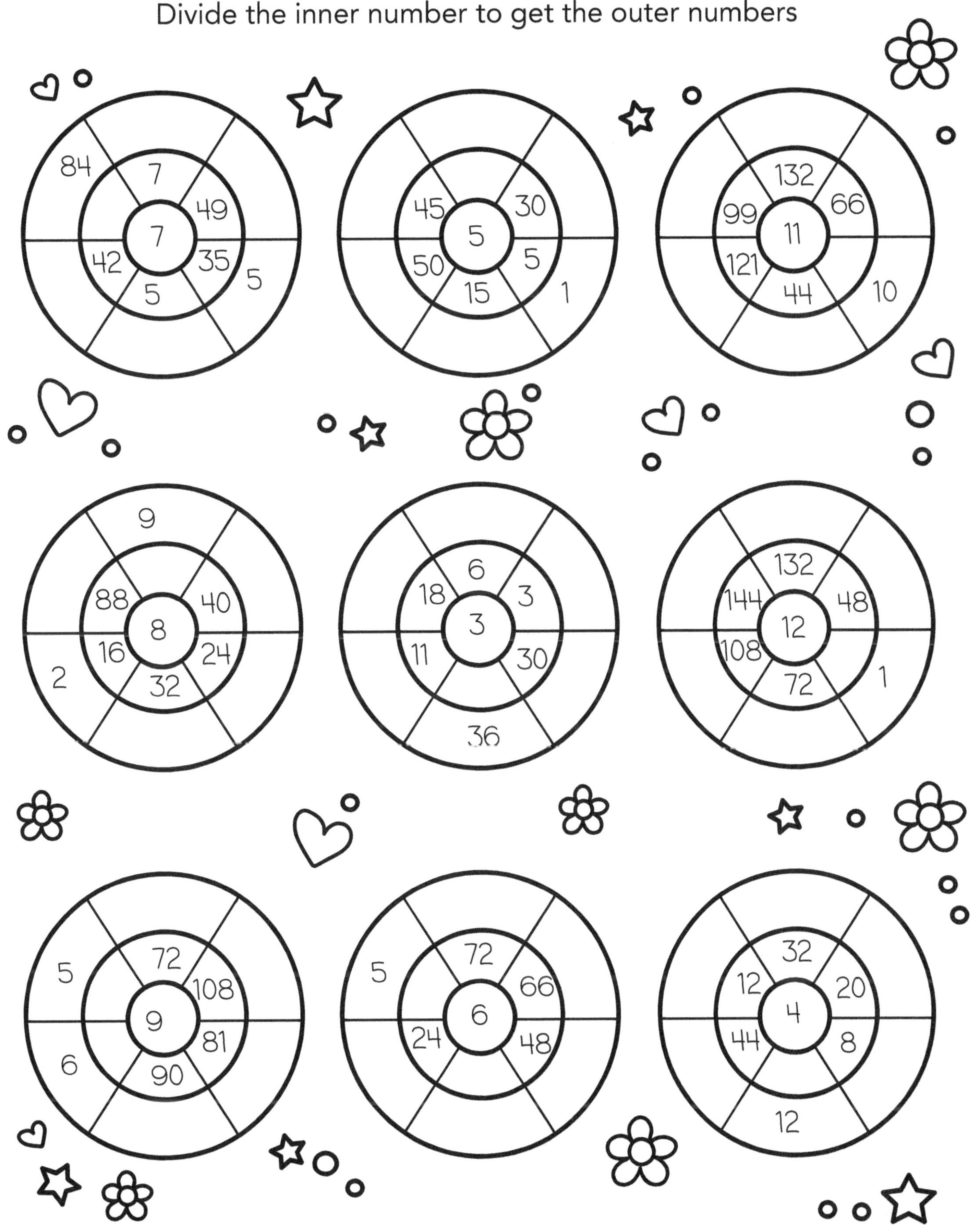

Division

Directions: Divide the numbers

50 ÷ 5	24 ÷ 4	18 ÷ 3	6 ÷ 2

12 ÷ 2	27 ÷ 3	40 ÷ 5	36 ÷ 4	22 ÷ 2

| 10 ÷ 5 | 28 ÷ 4 | 20 ÷ 2 | 32 ÷ 4 | 9 ÷ 3 |

| 44 ÷ 4 | 14 ÷ 2 | 21 ÷ 3 | 24 ÷ 2 | 35 ÷ 5 |

| 45 ÷ 5 | 2 ÷ 2 | 30 ÷ 5 | 33 ÷ 3 | 16 ÷ 4 |

| 36 ÷ 3 | 48 ÷ 4 | 60 x 5 | 15 ÷ 5 | 8 ÷ 4 |

Division

Directions: Divide the numbers

$36 \div 6 =$	$81 \div 9 =$	$36 \div 9 =$
$70 \div 7 =$	$24 \div 8 =$	$88 \div 8 =$
$32 \div 8 =$	$56 \div 7 =$	$42 \div 6 =$
$63 \div 9 =$	$66 \div 6 =$	$108 \div 9 =$
$28 \div 7 =$	$14 \div 7 =$	$78 \div 6 =$
$48 \div 8 =$	$9 \div 9 =$	$35 \div 7 =$
$90 \div 9 =$	$40 \div 8 =$	$96 \div 8 =$
$18 \div 6 =$	$72 \div 6 =$	$91 \div 7 =$

 # Division Maze 

Directions: Move left, right, up and down to follow the path of the TRUE division facts.

START	15÷5=4	12÷0=11	9÷9=81	1÷1=2
72÷6=12	9÷9=1	54÷6=8	42÷6=48	27÷3=8
10÷10=10	16÷4=4	36÷6=8	24÷8=4	4÷4=8
50÷3=10	66÷6=11	60÷12=11	14÷7=3	10÷5=3
21÷3=9	32÷4=8	48÷8=6	84÷8=12	63÷3=12
51÷6=9	66÷6=10	9÷3=3	10÷2=20	54÷9=7
11÷11=0	18÷3=3	25÷5=5	63÷9=7	81÷9=9
20÷10=3	35÷7=6	4÷2=1	33÷11=12	50÷5=10
45÷5=8	40÷8=7	48÷9=8	9÷3=11	12÷6=2
26÷3=8	34÷4=7	12÷6=3	80÷4=44	20÷4=5
4÷4=8	96÷6=12	2÷2=2	10÷2=3	END

Division Maze

Directions: Move left, right, up and down to follow the path of the TRUE division facts.

START	56÷8=12	24÷4=6	9÷9=81	1÷1=2
25÷3=5	12÷0=11	64÷8=8	49÷8=6	27÷3=8
99÷9=10	54÷6=8	108÷9=12	60÷6=5	70÷7=11
81÷9=8	36÷6=8	49÷7=7	14÷7=3	40÷5=9
40÷5=7	30÷3=10	10÷2=5	32÷2=12	63÷3=12
62÷7=9	18÷3=6	66÷6=10	72÷7=12	84÷12=8
36÷4=9	96÷12=8	35÷7=6	40÷8=48	64÷8=9
60÷10=3	56÷8=7	10÷2=12	4÷4=8	60÷12=11
18÷2=8	24÷12=2	36÷4=9	9÷3=11	12÷8=2
22÷2=9	34÷4=7	12÷12=1	80÷4=44	18÷3=3
33÷11=12	96÷6=12	END	10÷2=3	4÷1=5

Division Maze

Directions: Move left, right, up and down to follow the path of the TRUE division facts.

START	42÷7=6	49÷8=6	80÷4=44	72÷7=12
14÷7=3	22÷2=11	14÷7=2	18÷3=3	60÷6=5
32÷2=12	4÷1=5	84÷12=7	36÷6=8	12÷0=11
33÷11=12	81÷9=8	36÷6=6	27÷3=8	63÷3=12
88÷11=8	30÷3=10	45÷5=9	25÷3=5	99÷9=10
27÷9=3	40÷5=7	70÷7=11	40÷5=9	84÷12=8
35÷7=5	62÷7=9	96÷6=12	54÷6=8	9÷3=11
28÷7=4	4÷4=8	10÷2=12	60÷10=3	60÷12=11
63÷9=7	26÷3=8	18÷2=8	66÷6=10	35÷7=6
49÷7=7	34÷4=7	22÷2=9	1÷1=2	9÷9=81
6÷2=3	60÷5=12	110÷11=12	54÷6=9	END

Divide by 2's and 3's

Directions: Draw a line to match each equation

$16 \div 2$	2	$10 \div 2$
$6 \div 3$	12	$27 \div 3$
$24 \div 2$	7	$6 \div 2$
$15 \div 3$	9	$2 \div 2$
$14 \div 2$	8	$36 \div 3$
$9 \div 3$	1	$12 \div 3$
$18 \div 2$	5	$24 \div 3$
$3 \div 3$	11	$4 \div 2$
$8 \div 2$	3	$21 \div 3$
$33 \div 3$	6	$22 \div 2$
$12 \div 2$	10	$18 \div 3$
$30 \div 3$	4	$20 \div 2$

➗ DIVIDE BY 7 's and 8's ➗

Directions: Draw a line to match each equation

72÷8	9	84÷7
28÷7	1	21÷7
96÷8	10	64÷8
14÷7	3	35÷7
8÷8	4	63÷7
56÷7	12	48÷8
24÷8	7	32÷8
70÷7	2	88÷8
40÷8	11	16÷8
42÷7	5	49÷7
56÷8	8	7÷7
77÷7	6	80÷8

Division Crossword

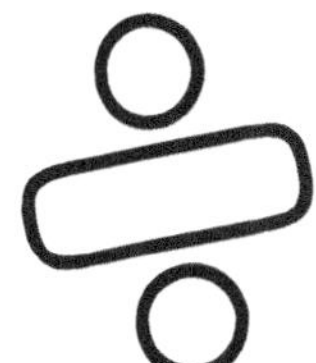

Directions: Fill in the blank to make the number sentence true

$$120 \div = 10$$

$$ \div 2 = 2 \div 2 = 1$$

$$ \div 6 = 5$$

$$2 \div = 1$$

$$15 \div 3 = $$

Vertical:

$$120 \div 2 = $$

$$10 \div 2 = = 1$$

$$2 \div 2 = 1$$

$$1 \div 1 = 1$$

$$ \div 2 = = 15$$

$$ \div 3 = $$

$$ \div 5 = 1$$

Division Crossword

Directions: Fill in the blank to make the number sentence true

108	÷	6	=	
		÷		÷
		2	9	÷	3
		=	=	-
60	÷		=	2
÷				=
	÷	2	=	1
=				
10	÷		=	2
		÷	÷	
		5	2	
		=	=	
		1		

Division Missing Factors

Directions: Fill in the missing division fact.

$36 \div \boxed{} = 6$

$44 \div \boxed{} = 4$

$96 \div \boxed{} = 12$

$64 \div \boxed{} = 8$

$18 \div \boxed{} = 2$

$42 \div \boxed{} = 7$

$88 \div \boxed{} = 11$

$25 \div \boxed{} = 5$

$6 \div \boxed{} = 1$

$21 \div \boxed{} = 3$

$81 \div \boxed{} = 9$

$100 \div \boxed{} = 10$

$24 \div \boxed{} = 12$

$9 \div \boxed{} = 3$

$40 \div \boxed{} = 8$

$72 \div \boxed{} = 9$

$2 \div \boxed{} = 1$

$33 \div \boxed{} = 11$

$20 \div \boxed{} = 4$

$45 \div \boxed{} = 5$

$14 \div \boxed{} = 2$

$54 \div \boxed{} = 6$

$49 \div \boxed{} = 7$

$30 \div \boxed{} = 10$

Division Missing Factors

Directions: Fill in the missing division fact.

80 ÷ [ ] = 10	99 ÷ [ ] = 11
48 ÷ [ ] = 8	12 ÷ [ ] = 3
24 ÷ [ ] = 6	32 ÷ [ ] = 4
4 ÷ [ ] = 2	35 ÷ [ ] = 5
16 ÷ [ ] = 4	84 ÷ [ ] = 7
120 ÷ [ ] = 12	55 ÷ [ ] = 5
8 ÷ [ ] = 1	32 ÷ [ ] = 8
15 ÷ [ ] = 5	108 ÷ [ ] = 12
63 ÷ [ ] = 9	90 ÷ [ ] = 10
28 ÷ [ ] = 7	18 ÷ [ ] = 9
30 ÷ [ ] = 3	9 ÷ [ ] = 1
22 ÷ [ ] = 11	20 ÷ [ ] = 2

Divide and Multiply

Directions: Solve the problems below, follow the example

Example:

$12 \div 2 = \boxed{6}$ because $6 \times 2 = 12$

$40 \div 10 = \boxed{}$ because _______________________

$35 \div 5 = \boxed{}$ because _______________________

$36 \div 6 = \boxed{}$ because _______________________

$24 \div 4 = \boxed{}$ because _______________________

$49 \div 7 = \boxed{}$ because _______________________

$64 \div 8 = \boxed{}$ because _______________________

$21 \div 3 = \boxed{}$ because _______________________

$18 \div 2 = \boxed{}$ because _______________________

$63 \div 9 = \boxed{}$ because _______________________

$33 \div 11 = \boxed{}$ because _______________________

Division equal groups

Directions: Write a division sentence to match the model.

_____ ÷ _____ = _____

_____ ÷ _____ = _____

_____ ÷ _____ = _____

_____ ÷ _____ = _____

_____ ÷ _____ = _____

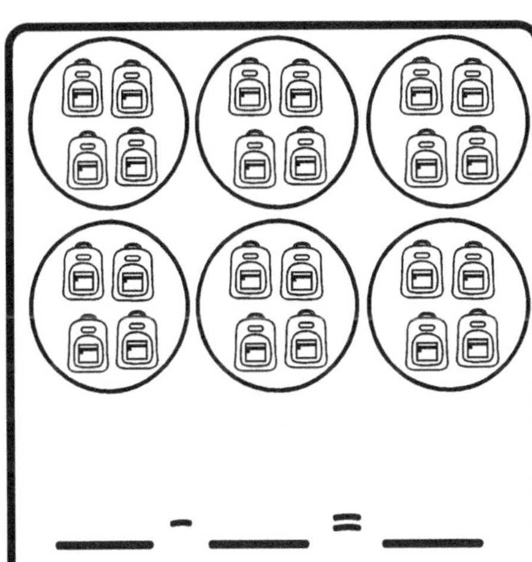

_____ ÷ _____ = _____

_____ ÷ _____ = _____

_____ ÷ _____ = _____

_____ ÷ _____ = _____

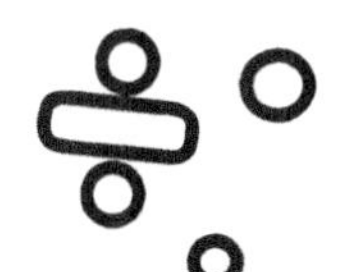 Division equal groups

Directions: Write a division sentence to match the model.

 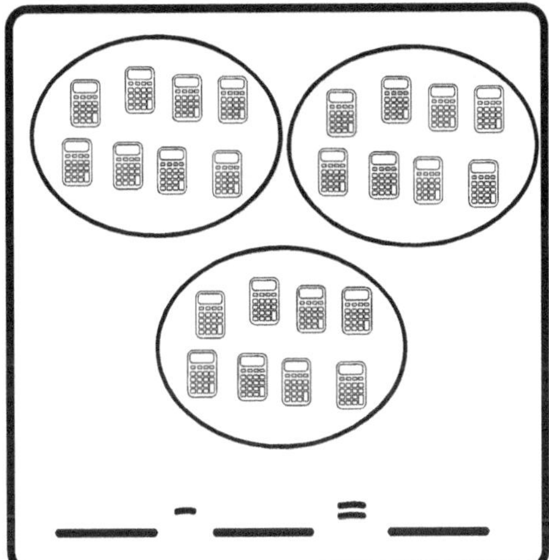 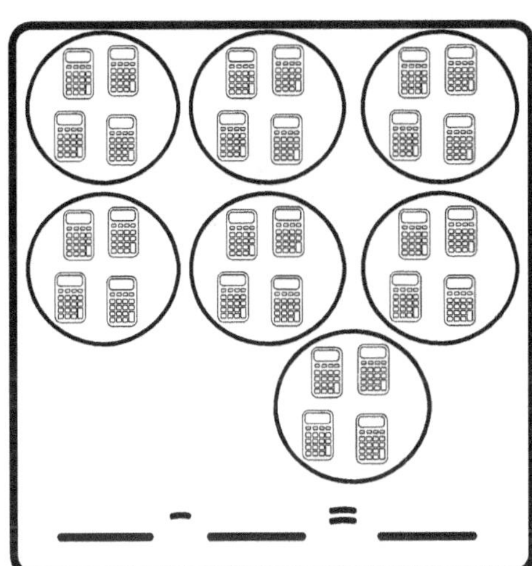

____ ÷ ____ = ____   ____ ÷ ____ = ____   ____ ÷ ____ = ____

 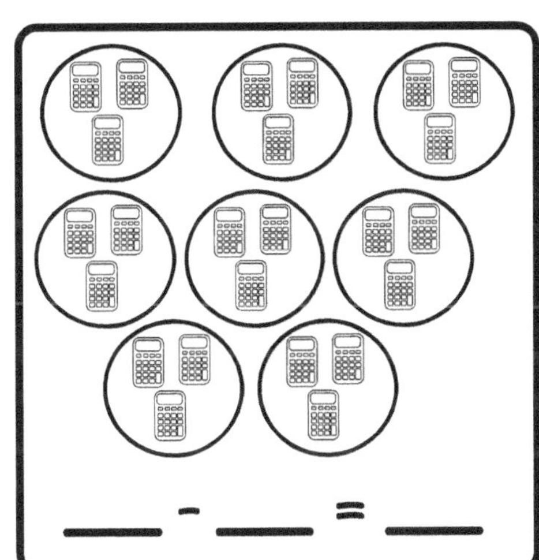 

____ ÷ ____ = ____   ____ ÷ ____ = ____   ____ ÷ ____ = ____

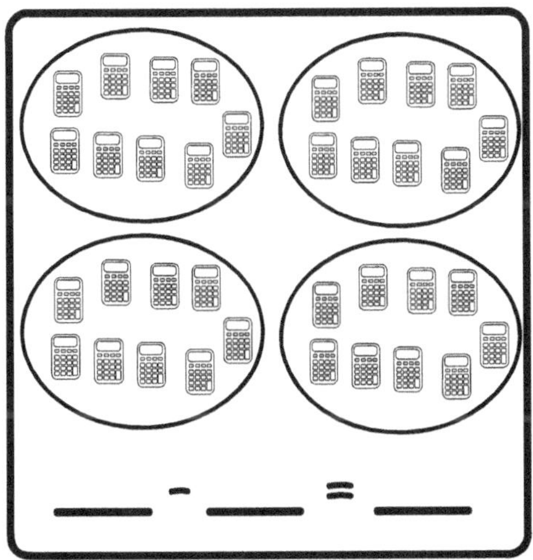 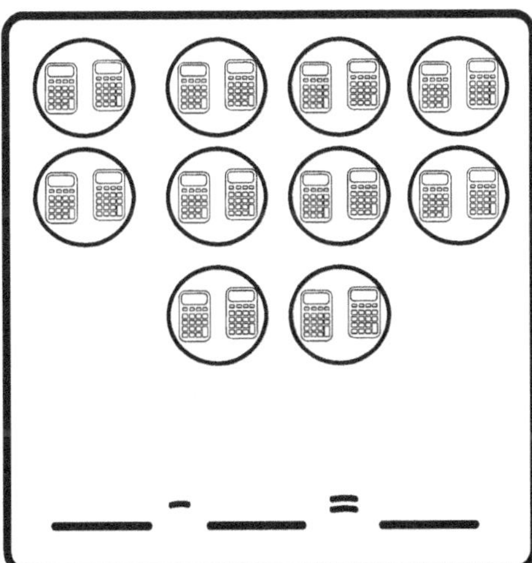 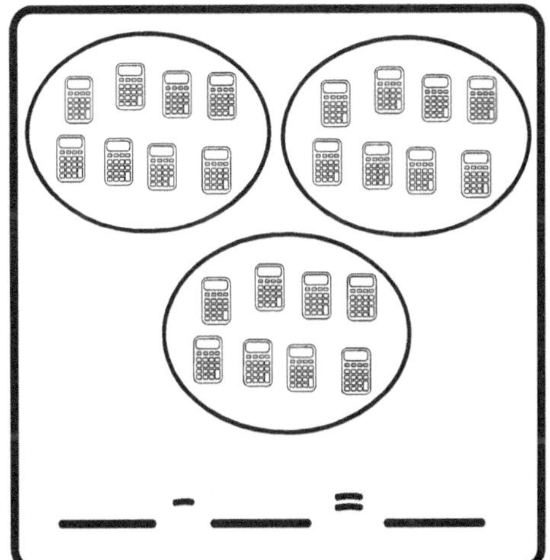

____ ÷ ____ = ____   ____ ÷ ____ = ____   ____ ÷ ____ = ____

Division equation

Directions: Circle the correct answer

$81 \div 9$

$88 \div 8$

$84 \div 7$

$50 \div 5$

$56 \div 7$

$54 \div 9$

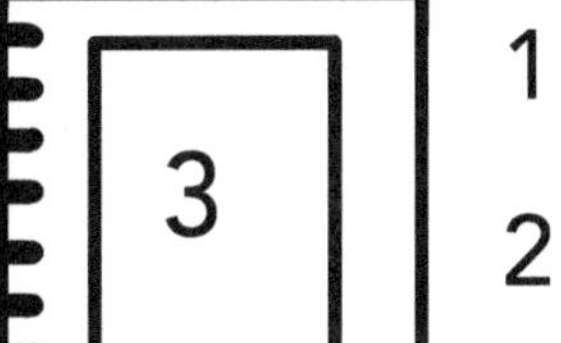

$15 \div 5$

$24 \div 6$

$10 \div 2$

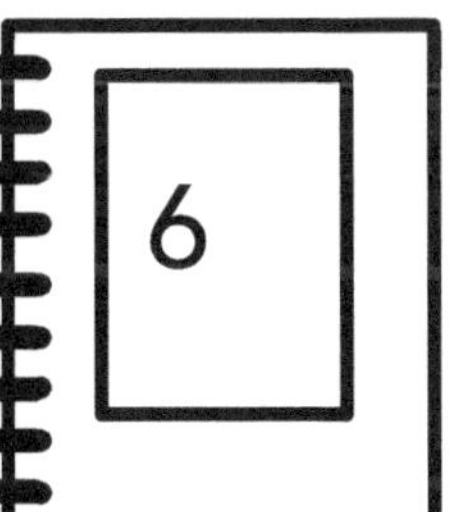

$35 \div 7$

$32 \div 8$

$36 \div 6$

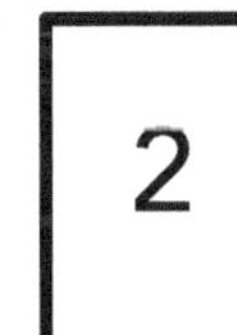

$18 \div 3$

$14 \div 7$

$16 \div 4$

$30 \div 6$

$10 \div 2$

$40 \div 4$

$36 \div 6$

$45 \div 9$

$33 \div 3$

$24 \div 3$

$20 \div 5$

$25 \div 5$

$72 \div 8$

$70 \div 10$

$77 \div 11$

$45 \div 9$

$48 \div 6$

$48 \div 7$

$54 \div 6$

$56 \div 8$

$55 \div 11$

$32 \div 4$

$35 \div 7$

$30 \div 5$